> **AN INTERACTIVE TOOL TO HELP YOU MANAGE YOUR FINANCES & CREATE AN EFFECTIVE BUDGET FOR YOUR FUTURE PLANS.**
>
> Ken Lindsey

# TABLE OF CONTENT

| | |
|---|---|
| Why Budget? | 04 |
| Why Budgets Fail? | 05 |
| Misconceptions about Money | 06 |
| Goals | 08 |
| Develop a Process | 11 |
| Establish a Foundation | 13 |
| Draw the Blueprint | 15 |
| Create Internal Controls | 21 |
| System Requirements | 23 |
| Perfecting Your Plan | 25 |
| Design Your Success | 26 |

# WHY BUDGET?

Budgeting is a financial tool that helps individuals manage their money. It is important to map out a process to help you determine what your financial journey will look like and give an idea of how long it will take you to get the results you want. Your budget (blueprint) is a great way to plan and successfully achieve your goals.

**Do you know where your money is going? Do you know how much money you could be saving each month?**

These are typical questions that most individuals don't know how to answer. If managing money was easy, there would be less debt and more goals accomplished. Planning is key and when we fail to plan, we lose sight of budgets.

Creating goals require planning. Let's look at some goals that many consumers dream about, but fail to accomplish because there's no budget.

### Goal: New Home
Proposed Plan: 20% down payment

### Goal: New Vehicle
Proposed Plan: Low interest rate or Payoff in two years or less

### Goal: Debt Free
Proposed Plan: Eliminate credit cards and Use Cash

### Goal: Live Life on Your Own Terms
Proposed Plan: Savings Plan, Retirement Plan, College Fund

> **LinZ View:**
> If the plan doesn't work, modify the plan, but never the goal.

# WHY **BUDGETS FAIL?**

To create an effective budget, you must first understand why budgets fail.

**01** **Unrealistic Projections**
Be honest with yourself! Make sure your expectations are realistic when creating a budget. Always keep the end goal in mind, but pace yourself. This is YOUR game plan for YOUR future!

Rome wasn't built in a day so leave room to grow. Don't create a budget based on where you want to be. Create a budget based on your current finances and expenses.

**02** **No Written Plan**
A written budget helps you stay on track. Keep your budget in a location where you can review on a weekly basis. Check off expenses as they are paid.

**03** **Forgotten Items**
Budgets often fail because individuals forget to include life events in their budget. What happens when life happens?

*Examples* include birthdays, graduations, weddings, car insurance, and/or property taxes. These items are not put in the monthly budget, but must be accounted for when creating a budget for short term savings *(see Step 5 for more details)*.

**List important dates that will occur in the next three months:**
Birthdays - Anniversaries - Graduations - Car Insurance - Property Taxes

| | Description | Date | | Description | Date |
|---|---|---|---|---|---|
| 1 | | | 4 | | |
| 2 | | | 5 | | |
| 3 | | | 6 | | |

**Did You Know?**

**You are more likely to achieve your plans if you write them down.**

## MISCONCEPTIONS ABOUT MONEY

The more money I have, the happier I'll be.
A bigger income will keep me out of debt.
The more money I have, the less worries I'll have.

There are many misconceptions about money; like money is the solution to everything. Of course more money may lead to an increase in happiness or a decrease in debt. The problem lies, however, with managing money. Without proper management, you can find yourself in more debt and the temporary happiness you once felt is now gone.

Money management is the one area consumers tend to fail, but it doesn't have to be that way. Discipline is key! If you learn how to manage $10, you will know how to manage $10,000. Budgeting is a financial tool that helps you manage your finances and teaches you how to get in front of your money and tell it where to go instead of grasping for it because it is constantly leaving you. The process isn't always easy, but it is necessary when you have an end goal in mind. Getting your finances in order will allow you to obtain your goals; one step at a time.

**Your only LIMIT is you.**

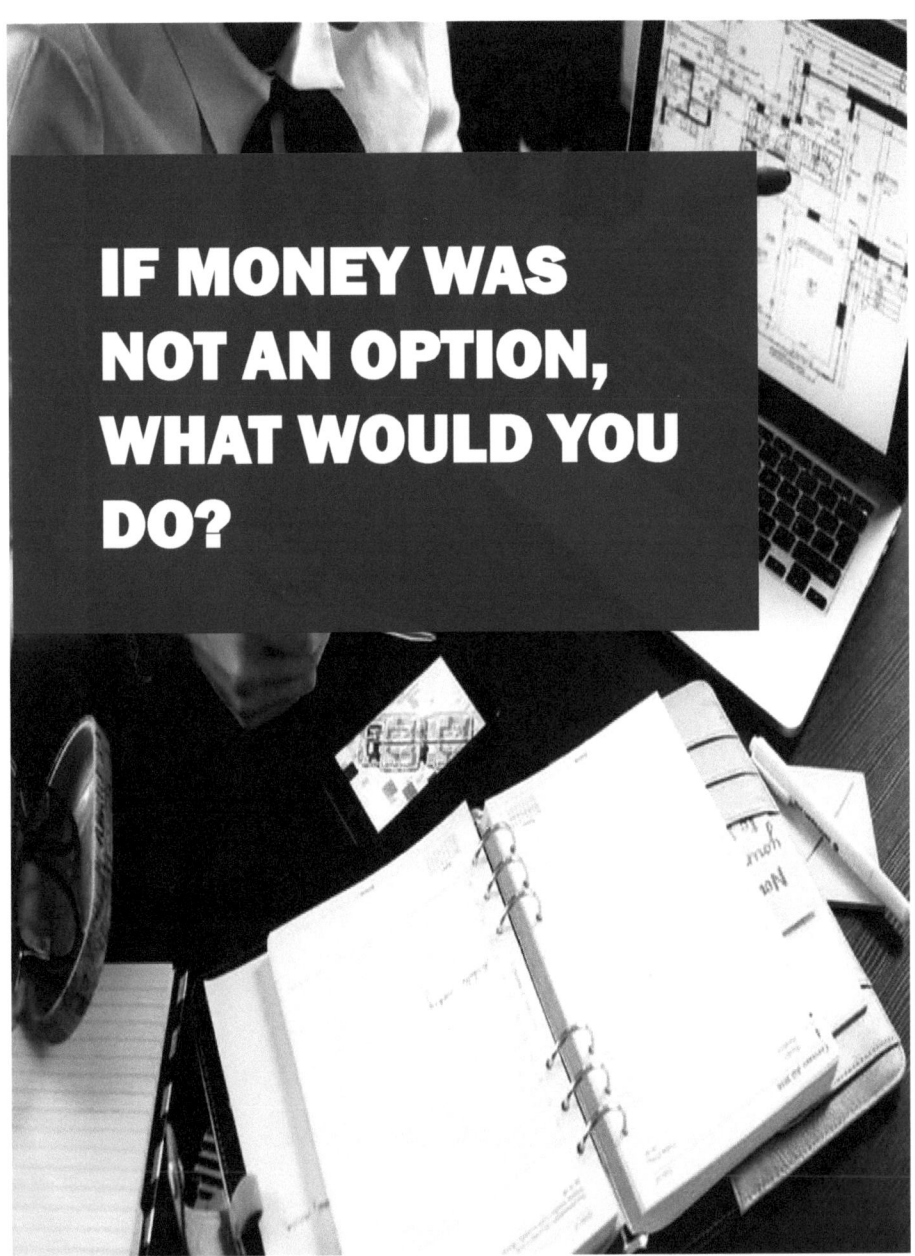

# GOALS

**If money was not an option, I would....**
(Take a moment and define your goals below.)

---

---

---

---

---

---

> **Setting goals is the first step in turning the invisible into the visible.**
>
> Tony Robbins

# BUDGETING
## IS A REPRESENTATION of.....

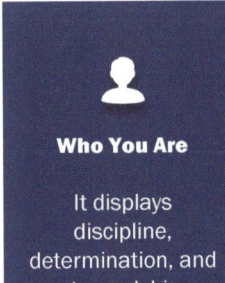
**Who You Are**
It displays discipline, determination, and stewardship.

**Where You Want to Go**
It fuels your future goals.

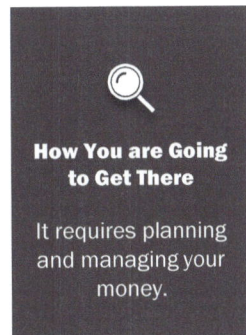
**How You are Going to Get There**
It requires planning and managing your money.

**Think of your plan from the previous page.**

It's time to create a budget that will help you achieve your goals

AND

Put an end to money myths.

**NOTES:**

# STEP 01
# DEVELOP A PROCESS

**Track Personal Spending**
To create an effective budget, study prior spending habits and develop a process. Get as much data as possible to ensure you understand all your financial responsibilities.

**Perception vs Reality**
**Perception**
How much money do you think you spend monthly in each category? Use the pie graph to the right to categorize these expenses.

Categories: Household, Debt, Food/Entertainment, Savings

Example:

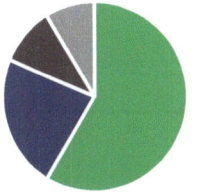

**Household**
**Debt**
**Food**
**Savings**

Your Household:

**Reality**
Budgets help you see exactly where your money goes. *(Get in front of it.)* Review your last three bank statements. How much money was spent on the following items?

| | | | |
|---|---|---|---|
| Mortgage | _____ | Entertainment | _____ |
| Utilities | _____ | Food | _____ |
| Clothing | _____ | Debt | _____ |
| Vehicle | _____ | Other | _____ |

## Track Personal Spending *continued...*

*Something to think about....*
Were you surprised about your findings?             Yes / No

### Why? Why not?

------------------------------------------------------------------------
------------------------------------------------------------------------
------------------------------------------------------------------------
------------------------------------------------------------------------
------------------------------------------------------------------------
------------------------------------------------------------------------

### Record the number of times your debit / credit card was used.  _____

What expenses can be eliminated right away? What areas do you see an opportunity to improve? Don't focus too much on where you've been or where you are. Use this exercise as a learning tool to where you are going.

------------------------------------------------------------------------
------------------------------------------------------------------------
------------------------------------------------------------------------
------------------------------------------------------------------------
------------------------------------------------------------------------
------------------------------------------------------------------------

**Did You Know?**

**Americans spend billions each year on fast food.**

# STEP 02
# ESTABLISH THE FOUNDATION

To establish a solid foundation, it is important to understand what you are building. Obstacles can destroy your foundation if they go unnoticed. There are four important metrics to creating a solid foundation: pay cycle, expense categories, due dates, debt.

### 1. Income: Know Your Income & Pay Cycles

a. Pay Cycle (weekly, bi-weekly, or monthly)

b. Other Sources of Income (alimony, child support etc.) _____

Determine an average income per pay period if your paychecks fluctuate. Always be conservative. If possible, do not depend on overtime or bonuses.

Income 1: Pay Cycle _____ Avg. Pay _____ (after taxes)

Income 2: Pay Cycle _____ Avg. Pay _____ (after taxes)

### 2. Classify All Expenses

Household – Transportation - Utilities – Debt – Other (non-essentials)
(More details on classifying expenses can be found in Step 3: Draw the Blueprint)

### 3. Due Dates

It is important to know all your due dates to avoid late fees and a poor reflection on your credit report. Avoid penalties and bank fees due to overdrafts.

### 4. Debt

Write down all your debt. Include current balances and minimum payments due.

# NOTES:

**LinZ View**

**Creating an effective budget requires understanding each process.**

# STEP 03
# DRAW THE BLUEPRINT

**Classify Expenses**
It is important to classify your expenses to understand essentials vs non-essentials *(needs vs. a want)*.

**Categories:** Household – Utilities – Transportation – Debt – Other

### 1. Household

- Mortgage / Rent
- Charity / Contributions
- Childcare
- Health / Life Insurance
- Grocery / Meals
- Savings

**Mortgage / Rent**
If you own your home, consider paying extra on the principal to reduce the # of years on your mortgage. Paying an extra $25 or $50 a month towards the principal will have a major impact long term and will reduce the amount of interest owed.

**Childcare**
Toddlers - includes daycare, diapers, and formula.
School Age - includes after school care, summer care / activities, and school lunch.

*Note: This category does not include extracurricular activities.*

## Classify Expenses *continued...*

### Savings
*See Step 5: System Requirements*

### Grocery/Meals
This category is the most common area to lose sight of expenses. Avoid using debit/credit cards to eliminate overspending. Carry cash when grocery shopping. Use leftover cash for quick trips to the grocery store to buy miscellaneous items.

> **LinZ View:**
> Pre-plan meals to avoid going over your budget when grocery shopping.

### 2. Transportation

Vehicle Payments  -  Insurance  -  Fuel

**Insurance**
- Research different Insurance companies to make sure you are getting the best deal.
- Reduce insurance premium by paying every six months or once a year. Ask your insurance provider if this option is available. Check for additional discounts.

**Fuel**
Set a weekly or bi-weekly budget for vehicle fuel. Using cash is the best option and reduces the chance of blowing your budget.

### 3. Utilities

| | |
|---|---|
| Gas | Telephone |
| Electric | Water |
| Cable / Internet* | Trash Services |

*Note: Cable/ Internet can be viewed as a "want". If your budget allows for this expense, include under utilities. Otherwise, classify under Other (non-essentials).*

### 4. Debt

| | |
|---|---|
| Personal or Student Loan | Medical |
| Credit Cards | Revolving Line of Credit |

**NOTES:**

## Classify Expenses *continued...*

List all known debt *(confirm with credit report)*.

| Company: | Balance: | Notes: |
|---|---|---|
| _____ | _____ | _____ |
| _____ | _____ | _____ |
| _____ | _____ | _____ |
| _____ | _____ | _____ |
| _____ | _____ | _____ |
| _____ | _____ | _____ |

### 5. Other (Non-Essentials)

Allowance  
Entertainment  
Miscellaneous  
Household

*Non-Essentials are entered last when creating a personal budget. Some non-essentials may have to be eliminated.

### Allowances *(personal care)*

Allowances are essential to budgeting. Everyone deserves one! Allowances reduce the amount of miscellaneous transactions that occur in the bank account. After all expenses have been accounted for, review the amount of excess funds each month. Allocate a portion to savings *(see Step 5)*. Then, create a budget for allowances to be used for individual personal care.

Always use cash for allowances! Withdraw the allowance budget out of the account. When it's gone; it's gone! Frequency of allowance should be determined by excess funds in the account (per pay cycle or monthly). *Examples include: haircare, clothing, feminine care, or personal entertainment.*

> **LinZ Recommendation:**
> Review your last three bank statements & determine the average amount of money spent each month on personal care. Is this amount affordable in your current budget?    Yes / No

The Blueprint to Financial Success: Budgeting

## Classify Expenses *continued...*

### Entertainment
Most people exclude entertainment in their budget, but it is a reality. No one wants to work hard and not play. Include entertainment to avoid blowing the budget. An entertainment budget is determined after a budget is created for savings and allowance. Examples of Entertainment include movies, dining out, and extracurricular activities. Use cash to avoid excess withdrawals from the bank account.

### Household Items
Household items include cleaning supplies, paper products & laundry items. *Do not include household items in the grocery budget.*

**Did You Know?**
If you have $20 in your pocket and no debt, you are wealthier than 25% of Americans?

# STEP 04
# CREATE INTERNAL CONTROLS

## Staying within Your Means

Internal controls (DISCIPLINE) help you create tools to increase effectiveness and efficiency in your budgeting process. Boundaries must be established.

### 1. Avoid using Debit / Credit Cards

Pay with cash as much as possible.

List current Credit Cards & Annual Percentage Rate

| Credit Card | Rate | Credit Card | Rate |
|---|---|---|---|
| _____ | _____ | _____ | _____ |
| _____ | _____ | _____ | _____ |

### 2. Equal Payment Plan - Utilities

Utilities fluctuate throughout the year.
Stabilize expenses as much as possible.
Contact utility companies to see if you qualify for equal payment plan.

| | |
|---|---|
| Electrical | yes / no |
| Water | yes / no |
| Gas | yes / no |

If equal payment plans are not available to you, take an average of the last 3 months to determine a budget.

*Note: These amounts will vary based on the seasons.*

### 3. Negotiate Due Dates (if applicable)

It is important to get all expenses in line with each pay cycle. If your credit is in good standing, some creditors will allow you to change your due dates. **ASK!!!**

Pay expenses early to avoid spending excess funds on unnecessary items.

---

**LinZ Recommendation:**
Great resource – www.creditkarma.com

## Staying within Your Means *continued...*

### 4. Base all expenses on a 4-week month.

\*\*only applies to individuals who are paid weekly or bi-weekly\*\*

If you are paid weekly or bi-weekly, you should receive 2 extra paychecks a year. If your budget is based on a 4-week month, these extra pay cycles should be allocated to Savings and Debt.

*Note: There will be some expenses incurred during "extra" pay cycles (i.e. groceries, fuel).*

### 5. Budget for Special Occasions

Discipline is KEY! Have a budget within your budget for special occasions. Determine an amount to be spent on Special Occasions. Then, allocate as needed.

On average, what do you / your spouse typically spend on individual gifts?
_____

List special occasions and determine a reasonable budget for each:

| Description | Amount | Description | Amount |
|---|---|---|---|
| 1. | | 4. | |
| 2. | | 5. | |
| 3. | | 6. | |

**LinZ Recommendation:**
When overtime or bonuses are received, allocate a portion to debt and deposit the rest in savings. Do not rely on additional income as it is not always guaranteed.

# STEP 05
# SYSTEM REQUIREMENTS

## Pay Yourself

An essential part of the blueprint is system requirements. In order to support your goals, you have to pay yourself **(save)** in the budgeting process.

## Savings

After all expenses have been accounted for, it is important to pay yourself before creating a budget for expenses in the "Other" category (i.e. entertainment, allowances, etc.). Most consumers put savings last on the list. As a result, saving for the future sometimes never happen. Treat your savings like a bill and "pay" it every month like other expenses.
*(Savings are included in the household category on your budget.)*

## Goals

Save at least 10% of your income monthly (excluding retirement options). Create three types of Savings: Short Term - Long Term - Other

### Short Term Savings
- Account can be at the same bank institution as checking account.
- Account is to be used for vacations, birthdays, major holidays, car maintenance, or minor life events.
- 35% of monthly savings is allocated to SHORT TERM Savings.

*Example:*
If your budget allows for your household to save $200 a month, allocate $70 to short term savings and $130 to long term savings. ($200 x .35 = $70)

### Long Term Savings
- Set up account at a different bank institution (no easy access).
- 65% of monthly savings is allocated to Long Term Savings.
- Account to be used for investments and major purchases (i.e. house, vehicle etc.)
- Long Term Goal: Save enough to cover three months of expenses.

### Other Savings
Employer 401k, IRA, Stocks, Investments.

## NOTES:

---

**LinZ Recommendation:**
Research local bank institutions, credit unions, or financials service centers to get more information on Certificate of Deposits, Money Markets, IRAs, or other investment opportunities.

# PERFECTING YOUR PLAN

If you create a budget and stick to it, you are less likely to blow your money. Learn to say NO!

Budgets help you....

1. know who you are paying and how much you are spending.
2. stay focused on end goal.
3. identify and understand needs vs wants *(essentials vs non-essentials)*.
4. save

**Update Your Budget when....**

New expenses are identified            Debt is eliminated
Pay increases / decreases              Strain on the finances

### Do a Trial Run

Effective budgets are reviewed and updated on a quarterly basis. Establish a trial run for your new budget. Evaluate your progress and make sure you are getting the results you need.

- What worked?
- What didn't?
- What adjustments are needed?

# DESIGN YOUR SUCCESS

Now that you have established a solid foundation, drawn your blueprint, created controls, and identified system requirements, it's time to:

### Establish a New Mindset
Stick to your Blueprint.
Be Consistent.

### Implement the Plan
Be sure to communicate the changes to those involved (spouse/children). Establish an accountability partner.

If you don't have defined goals, your budget will soon lose its direction. Get in front of your money and tell it where to go. Don't find yourself always chasing behind your money and trying to hold on to it. Budgets work if you want them to work.

"Don't invest in the outcome. Invest in the process."

**Dr. Srikumar Rao**

## READY, SET, GO.....

**Do you have a clear idea of where you want to go?**

Every household needs to create a blueprint (budget) that works for them. It can only be achieved by being disciplined, having goals, and a desire to do something different.

**NOTES:**

# NOTES:

---------------------------------------------------------------------

---------------------------------------------------------------------

---------------------------------------------------------------------

---------------------------------------------------------------------

---------------------------------------------------------------------

---------------------------------------------------------------------

Money does matter. How important is it to you?
For more information or to receive budget templates, contact info@linzfinancials.com.

No part of this book may be reproduced or transmitted in any form or by any means, electronic or mechanical, including photocopying, recording or by any information storage and retrieval system, without written permission from the author. The information contained within this book is strictly for educational purposes. If you wish to apply ideas contained in this book, you are taking full responsibility for your actions.

www.ingramcontent.com/pod-product-compliance
Lightning Source LLC
Chambersburg PA
CBHW040304220526
45473CB00002B/580